ARISE DEVOTIONAL BOOK

ARISE DEVOTIONAL BOOK

Arise to the New in Christ

Elder Felicia Edmond

ARISE DEVOTIONAL BOOK

Published by AGD Publishing Services

Unless otherwise indicated, scripture quotations are from The Holy Bible, King James Version.

Printed in the United States of America

Paperback ISBN: 978-1-7372867-4-5
eBook ISBN: 978-1-7372867-5-2

CONTENTS

DEDICATION

This book is dedicated to all who look forward to arising to new levels and have no limits to what they will experience in Christ

Arise, Shine for Your light has come, And the Glory of the Lord is risen upon you Isaiah 60:1

A special dedication to my husband Jerry. Thank you for always loving me, supporting me, and cheering me on. Your love for me is Heaven Sent.

ACKNOWLEDGEMENTS

Thanks to my family, my husband Jerry, my children Joelle and Jonathan for always surrounding me with love, joy and continuous support.

A special thanks to my late father Sherman, my mother Doris, siblings Gordon, Darlene, and Theresa and all my nieces and nephews, in-laws, and extended family

Thanks to all my beautiful friends and sisters-in-Christ. We always pray, encourage each other, and have each other's back. I am truly grateful!

Thanks to my very special mentor, Pastor Sonja Mahoney. Thank you for allowing God to use you in my life through pouring into me, sharing wisdom, and always reminding me of my purpose in Christ.

Thanks to my Pastor and church family for your support.

Thanks to my publisher, Reverend Allison G. Daniels and her team for helping this book become a reality in my life so that I can further reach others for the Lord

APPRECIATION POEMS

MOM, YOU ARE TREASURED

Mom, your love has always been clear

In fact, your love has always been near and dear

You have always sacrificed so, so much

Thus, to ensure our dreams could appear

You lovingly birthed and raised four

And along with Christ, it was your husband and
children you adore.

You were firm, but peaceful and calm

Your insight and strength helped us along.

Yes, along this road of life, your wisdom still comes to
mind

As I am encounter life's challenges and oh, the
rewarding times.

You are a strong example of a mother's love and embrace,

And you still continually pray for us, and you still seek
God's face.

You extend that love with excitement to your
grandchildren, as you pray and give

God's love and strength, you , truthfully live.

OUR DAUGHTER

You our beloved daughter, are beautiful
Look who you have become
And it still does not yet fully appear
All that He has promised and prepared
And your relationship with God, keeps drawing ever so near.
Oh yes, this is the victory that overcomes the world –even your faith
You are beautifully triumphantly running Your race.
You are victorious and a young woman of noble character we see
You will help to inspire, encourage many people
God has your wonderful destiny in view.
Yes, Glory to God, you do have a testimony to tell
How you have triumphantly persevered.
You've truly drank from His well.
You are already accepted in Christ
Continue to receive His favor and grace
For He will catapult you into His abundant life

OUR SON

Remember you are fearfully and wonderfully created by
God
and you my love, are His workmanship to do a great
work.
I just knew you had greatness, even before your birth
Oh yes, we know, through Jesus Christ, many battles you
have won
In the midst of trials, you persevere with laughter
and to the family you bring fun.
Oh how we love your reverence for God's Word
My son, always remember, God's Word is your sword
You speak His truth – it'll keep you free.
You're destined to have good success by helping many
And always remember you'll have sweet victory.

ARISE

Arise and shine for your light has come

Realize the victory has already been won

Do not fret and do not dread

Remember your best days are still ahead

It's truly time to shine and arise

With great anticipation, Look up and see, from God's view

That you are already in the new

This is now your set time

You must press forward and leave the past behind

You have a beautiful work to do

Rise up and break forth!

Remember He lovingly placed you on the Earth

It is your season to birth! Arise!

ALREADY MADE NEW

You are already made new

So why do you look back at what use to be

You must now realize you have a new identity.

You are a new creation in Christ Jesus, you see

You must forget what is behind and press toward the mark

of the high calling of God in Christ.

Jesus the Christ has given you a new life

So, when the enemy tries to remind you of failures from the past

Decree, declare and confess "I am God's beloved and only

what I do for Christ will last."

Stop repeating the old story and realize you are in the new

You have been made whole, it has transformed you into His image

Now daughter of the King, only see yourself from God's view

You are already made new.

A TIME OF REFLECTION

Identify any ways in which you still see yourself from your past with limitations.

Reflect on who you are as a new creation in Christ and name some of the gifts that He has put on the inside of you.

Note down in your journal the one practice you can put in place to remind yourself that you are a new creation and that you will let go of any limitations from the past.

LET US PRAY

Heavenly Father, thank you for making me a new creation in You. I receive all that You have for me in this season. Please help me to focus on my identity in You and the gifts You put on the inside of me. I am so excited about the new, in You. I release every limitation to You, and I declare my victory, in Jesus' name.

Colossians 3:10 "And have put on the new man, which is renewed in knowledge after the image of him that created him:"

AWAKENED TO THE NEW

I have awakened to the new
I am focusing only on God's view.
Circumstances may arise but are subject to change

He has wonderfully called me by name.
So, I must do what He has called me to do
to accomplish His will upon the earth
So that the vision He has given me will be birthed
For so long I was going through the motions and trusting in man
Now I have been awakened to God's perfect plan
God's plan for me is beautiful, in abundance and blessed
Even though in this life I have endured trials and many tests
In my newfound life, I will now focus on receiving God's

best
Thank You Lord, for awakening me to the new.

A TIME OF REFLECTION

Identify one thing God is leading you to do to focus on receiving God's best for your life?

What test or trial have you overcome recently that God has brought you through?

Identify one new thing you will embark upon this week towards God's plan for your life.

LET US PRAY

Heavenly Father I Thank You. I am so excited for the new. Thank You Lord for bringing me through every trial and tribulation. Dear Lord, I do receive Your best. Please remove all the doubts and all the unbelief. Thank you, Lord, that I am now awakened to the new, in Jesus' name. Amen!

Isaiah 52:1 "Awake, awake; put on thy strength, O Zion; put on thy beautiful garments, O Jerusalem, the holy city: for henceforth there shall no more come into thee the uncircumcised and the unclean."

3

THE NEW ME, THE NEW YOU

They thought I was timid, stuck, and afraid, but look at
The Price My Jesus paid.
The new me was there all along. I just didn't know how to
sing the new song.
God used authentic people to see the beauty in me

While others questioned my destiny.
They didn't realize that man looks at the outward
appearance

But God looks at the heart.
You see, His mercies are new every morning, so there is
always an opportunity for a new start
Remember to embrace the new creation that you are
For the blessings He has for you are near
What our Heavenly Father has for you is never far
Now, despite what anyone else says, focus on His

promises for you,
Look at His thoughts and His ways; His Word to you will
never return void
This abundant life You truly can enjoy.
Don't identify with the negative words spoken over you;
speak God's Word over your life
Before the foundation of the world, God already knew
the new you.

A TIME OF REFLECTION

What have you learned from your journey of life about embracing the new that God has for you?

Dream Big! What is God putting in your heart to look forward to in life?

Please, journal your thoughts as you reflect upon yourself as a new creation in Christ.

LET US PRAY

Heavenly Father I come in Jesus' name worshipping You. Thank You for dying on the cross for me and making me a new creation in You. Help me Lord to embrace who You have created me to be. Help me to forget those things that are behind and move forward and look forward to the newness in Christ, for me, in Jesus' name. Amen.

Philippians 3:13 "Brethren, I count not myself to have apprehended: but this one thing I do, forgetting those things which are behind, and reaching forth unto those things which are before,"

4

CONSISTENT LOVE

Jesus Your love is the most consistent love I know

As I look all around Your love still flows

Through betrayals, hurts and disappointment from others

I realize now that You are the friend who sticks closer than a brother

Your love heals every pain and hurt

Your love makes me alive and new

Your love is unconditional, consistent, and true

You showed Your love at Calvary when You made the choice to die, and then resurrect for me

You gave me fresh sight, new lenses to see

Your love helps me to forgive, live, love and be free

You heal the brokenhearted and You also are the lifter of my head

I no longer look back I press forward looking ahead

Those betrayals, hurts and disappointments are forgiven and are now in the past

I am delivered and now focused on Your true consistent love which lasts

I am truly new; I've been set free; I receive Your love Lord with sweet liberty.
With sweet freedom, I love myself and others, and I gracefully embark upon this newfound journey.

A Time of Reflection

Reflect for a few moments on the time in your life where you know the love of God brought you through a situation.

What are some ways you will focus on the love of God in your life? For example, do you play worship songs and reflect on scriptures of His love.

Please spend time journaling about how much God loves you.

LET US PRAY

Heavenly Father Your love towards me is significant in my life. Thank You, Lord. Your love is the foundation for my life. Please help me to encounter Your love in a tangible way, each and every day. Help me to allow Your love to heal me in places where I am experiencing hurt. Help me to focus on Your love, in the name of Jesus I pray. Amen.

Ephesians 3:18-19 "May be able to comprehend with all saints what is the breadth, and length, and depth, and height; 19 And to know the love of Christ, which passeth knowledge, that ye might be filled with all the fulness of God."

FOLLOW HIS VOICE

At times in life, I may be given a choice,

But I must always all the time, follow His Voice.

In life there are so many decisions to make

I ask myself many times, what does it take?

It takes courage, wisdom, and peace.

Now I can clearly see the way to go,

Sometimes, however, fear has stopped me, this I know.

Oh there have been many times I have followed the crowd

Even though my Savior spoke to me so gentle and dear

I wanted acceptance, I wanted applause, I wanted love,

But clearly, I see that the love was already there from Heaven above.

You see it was on the inside of me where the Holy Spirit abides,

I must always follow His voice because He truly is my guide.

Oh, but what if I lose people, my friends and acceptance along the way

He tells me, I will take care of you and perfect that which concerns you, I hear my Lord say

God says to me, "follow Me I am the way"

Truly, He is the way, the truth and the life

When I follow Him, I walk with clear vision and sight

I know that He is the One who tremendously gives me the abundant life.

A Time of Reflection

What is God speaking to you in this season?

What was a time in your life where you followed God instead of the crowd?

What steps will you make towards following what God is speaking to your heart in this season?

Let Us Pray

Heavenly Father help me to focus and listen to hear and follow Your voice. Please help me to be obedient to You, to follow Your will. With You, Lord, all things are possible, and I truly know that the best –Your best is yet to come. I am excited about Your plans for me Dear Lord, in Jesus' name I pray. Amen.

John 10:27 "My sheep hear my voice, and I know them, and they follow me:"

6

WISDOM FROM ABOVE

And why do I fight,

When in my heart, I know Dear Lord You have given me profound insight.

You have the answers to every problem I face,

As I turn to Your Word You show me how to run this race.

You tell me to be still and know that You are God

You tell me to ask for wisdom which You always give liberally

So why would I try to figure it out on my own?

When You said I could come boldly to the throne of grace,

I can seek first Your Kingdom and freely seek Your face.

Each day, each moment I must decide that I must truly in You abide.

As I abide in You and hear only Your voice

I know that I am making the right choice.

You said that You will work all things out for our good

I will cling to You Lord as I have now understood

The righteous are never forsaken

Nor our seed begging for bread

As we focus on Your Word Dear Lord,

Our best days are not behind but they are surely ahead.

A Time of Reflection

What areas in your life have you been seeking the wisdom of the Lord?

What areas of your life do you need to seek the wisdom of the Lord that you have not yet surrendered?

Please reference at least one scripture, make note of it to address an area in your life of which you need to surrender to the Lord.

LET US PRAY

Heavenly Father I thank You for being my source, my only source, in every area of my life. I need You in every decision that I make. Father help me to seek You daily and ask for Your wisdom. Thank You, Lord, for being my everything. Help me to stop figuring things out in my own strength but to totally lean on and depend on You, in Jesus' name I pray. Amen.

James 1:5-6 "If any of you lack wisdom, let him ask of God, that giveth to all men liberally, and upbraideth not; and it shall be given him. 6 But let him ask in faith, nothing wavering. For he that wavereth is like a wave of the sea driven with the wind and tossed."

7

TAKE THE NEXT STEP

You are called and chosen in Him,
You must realize in this call, that you win
Take the next step toward your destiny
So do not quit and do not fear
Your time, your season is now here
You may think you are not qualified
That you are not ready to begin, look forward, take the next step, take it in Him
It is not only for your win but also for someone else's win
He qualified you and equipped you for His abundance in this life
Eyes have not seen nor has it entered into the heart of man, what God has prepared for you
Keep your eyes on Him and keep the pursuit
Every day when you wake up and hear His voice
Embrace His unfailing love and make a choice

Take the next step in Him and remember His love for you
never ends.

A TIME OF REFLECTION

What is the next step you can or will take towards what God has prepared for you?

What are ways that you can help others as you reach your destiny?

What are ways in which you can focus on hearing God's voice during this season?

LET US PRAY

Heavenly Father I come to You in Jesus' name focusing on You and depending on You. Lord, please help me to take the next step in what You have prepared for me. Help me Lord to pursue You, and I desire to pursue You more than ever before. Lord, I give You all my fears and cares. Thank You, Lord, for helping me to overcome everything that is hindering me from having a closer, more intimate walk with You, in Jesus' name I pray. Amen.

Psalm 37: 23 "The steps of a good man are ordered by the Lord: and he delighteth in his way."

8

LETTING GO

God says come with me into the new and let go of the past,

I respond, "God I want to trust You but will this new way last?"

I have gone through many hurts before, and I have endured many disappointments

I have encountered many fears, so I want to feel safe in the things I know.

Lord, I know the familiar places and I trust my comfort zone,

But Jesus says, "follow me my child", as I make intercessions for you on the throne.

I began to see that God is an ever-present help and will be with me always

His mercies are new every morning and each day for me is a new day

I began to yield to God each moment, each day and I listen clearly to what my Savior says

So then, finally, I realized I must let go and embrace the new,

I must elevate my vision and see from God's point of view.

He said forget those things which are behind and do not remember the former things of old

Now I see I can truly let go and walking with Christ I can be bold.

God has prepared so much for me, the blessings of God are earnestly upon me,

I can now look ahead and now I can let go.

Because I see and I know that God does exceedingly abundantly, and in Him, we always grow,

So I will embrace the new, I will release the old and I watch the beautiful plan of God unfold.

A TIME OF REFLECTION

What is God leading you or ministering to you to really let go of during this season, for example, concerning relationships, places, or habits?

What is the first step you can, or you will make in moving out of your comfort zone and what is that one thing God is asking you to do to move out of your comfort zone?

In what area of your life do you need to yield to God even the more?

LET US PRAY

Heavenly Father, I come in the name of Jesus, thanking You for the newness in my life, which is a better life, a richer life in You. Lord, thank You for continuing to help me to let go of my past and embracing the new things You have in store for me. Help me to walk in *the blessing* You have for me. Thank You for delivering me from my fears. Thank You, Lord, for moving in my life in a mighty way, in Jesus' name I pray. Amen.

Isaiah 43:18-19 "Remember ye not the former things, neither consider the things of old.

Behold, I will do a new thing; now it shall spring forth; shall ye not know it? I will even make a way in the wilderness, and rivers in the desert."

9

LIVE FREE

We Live Free and release our pain,
We look to Him and call upon His name.
We know that there is true freedom in Christ,
We look forward to enjoying this abundant life.
We forget those things that are behind
And we press toward the high calling mark,
It is on this Jesus journey that you must continue to embark.
When things look bleak, we keep moving forward.
You know in your heart your sweet victory is assured.
So why are you cast down and filled with doubt?
Please, stay in His presence as His will, truly will come about.
Live Free in Christ and enjoy this set time,
God is doing a new thing and we must connect to Jesus, the true Vine.
Doubt, unbelief, and fear must be released,

Because where the Spirit of the Lord is, there is liberty,
Through Jesus Christ, you can truly Live Free.

A TIME OF REFLECTION

Is there anything hindering you now from living free in Christ?

What are some ways you can encourage yourself in the Lord?

Please journal and reflect upon what it looks like for you, personally, to be free in Christ.

LET US PRAY

Heavenly Father I come in Jesus' name thanking You for freedom. I release anything that is hindering my deliverance. Thank You, Lord, for Your victory. Help me to stay in Your presence and focus on You, I thank You, Lord, that I am now delivered and free in Jesus' name. Amen.

John 8:36 "If the Son therefore shall make you free, ye shall be free indeed."

10

THERE IS FREEDOM IN FORGIVENESS

I forgave out of love and obedience so now I am free,

The pain no longer has control of me.

Out of the abundance of His mercy and the abundance of His grace, I let it go,

Through the blessed assurance of Jesus Christ, I can now in Him mature and grow.

The chains are broken off my life,

Because I decided to forgive and let go of strife.

I had to surrender to Jesus, the Christ for my wellness and my total healing,

And now each day I can see what God is revealing.

When I look at those who I have forgiven,

I can now see them through the eyes of His love,

All because Christ has forgiven me, I must seek the heavenly things above

Unforgiveness no longer can hold me down

I can freely lift my hands in worship because Jesus' Agape love now flows all around.

A Time of Reflection

Please, ask God to reveal to you anyone you need to forgive.

Please, reflect upon how you can see others through the eyes of Christ.

Please, be committed to your journaling; ask the Lord to help you to release any unforgiveness you might be harboring –intentionally or unintentionally.

LET US PRAY

Heavenly Father, I come in the name of Jesus thanking You for forgiving me. Thank You, Lord for Your Agape love. Thank You, Lord, for giving me the grace to forgive others. Lord thank You for helping me to forgive, not in my own strength but out of the love and forgiveness You have given me. Father, I am grateful in Jesus' name. Amen.

Ephesians 4:32 "And be ye kind one to another, tenderhearted, forgiving one another, even as God for Christ's sake hath forgiven you."

11

MY SOURCE

Jesus, You are my source, and You supply my every need

You are always faithful to counsel and to comfort me

I looked to others to fill the void,

But then I finally realized You are the only One who truly brings peace and joy

You are there for me every moment and even in the midnight hour

You My Lord are my refuge and my strong tower

When I stopped looking to others and I began to look to You

My life now is exuberant, hopeful, I'm now elevated with a glorious point of view

You came to give me life and life more abundantly

Thank You Jesus because I am truly experiencing You and I am now free

I dare not look to another source

You are my Creator, and You know me better than I know myself

You knew me before the foundation of the world, even before my birth

Jesus Jesus Jesus, You truly are my only source.

A Time of Reflection

Identify, reflect on one time in your life where you saw God's faithfulness.

Meditate, please, on this question for a few moments and identify a source, name, something, anything in your life other than Christ in which you may be currently depending upon that you feel, or think is your source.

Now, please release the areas from question 2 to the Lord and reflect upon God being your source –your only source.

LET US PRAY

Heavenly Father, I thank You for being my source. Lord, You are my refuge. You are my shelter. You are lifted up in my life. Please help me, Lord, to put You first in every area of my life. Lord, I totally depend on You in the name of Jesus.

Acts 17:28 "For in him we live, and move, and have our being; as certain also of your own poets have said, For we are also his offspring."

12

GOD'S VALIDATION

I am accepted in the beloved

I am chosen of God by Him

I am not defeated; ultimately, I win

My validation comes from the inside

Where the Holy Spirit richly abides

Regardless of a title, status, or fame

I am truly validated by His name

He has given me His stamp of approval

Because of His unconditional love for me

Even when my name is not called upon by man

I have been assured, that I am still truly free

My name is written in the most important book

Which is the book by God and His outlook

So, as long as my name is written in the Lamb's Book of Life

My life every day is lived for Christ

It is the good fight of faith that I fight

One day I long to hear my Savior say well done

Because my daughter since you have accepted my victory on the cross

And you have accepted my resurrection power, you my daughter, have already won.

A Time of Reflection

Identify any challenges you are currently facing that gives you the feeling that you are not validated.

Please know, that our validation comes from our relationship with God, and from Him alone. Identify or write down any scriptures that might help you focus on your relationship with God.

Name three uplifting words to describe how God sees you.

LET US PRAY

Heavenly Father I come in the name of Jesus to thank You for being my Father and validating me. You are my Creator, My Lord, and my Savior. Help me to see myself as You see me, beautiful, loved and accepted. Thank You, Lord, for all that You have done for me, in Jesus' name I pray. Amen.

Psalm 139:13-14 "For thou hast possessed my reins: thou hast covered me in my mother's womb. 14 I will praise thee; for I am fearfully and wonderfully made: marvellous are thy works; and that my soul knoweth right well."

13

BEFORE THE FOUNDATION OF THE WORLD

Oh, how He loves us, yes, He chose us,

He created us in Him, to be holy and without blame, in Him

Before the foundation of the world, it all began.

We are His masterpiece, created for good works,

Oh yes, He ordained us even before our births.

Because of the blood, we are brought near to Christ,

In His presence, we experience abundant life.

We realize that He has a great purpose and plan,

His promises are Yes and Amen!

His thoughts toward us are of love, peace, and hope.

His kindness towards us will never depart,

And to realize just how much He knows us best,

He continues to love on us, and He orders our steps

We must pursue God with our whole heart.

A Time of Reflection

You are created by God, in His image, so please list some ways you are uniquely gifted by Him.

Reflect on a time in your life where you can see the plan of God unfolding, coming together for you.

Identify a current area in your life where you see God moving in your life.

LET US PRAY

Heavenly Father, thank You for saving me and that You knew me before I was formed in my mother's womb. Please help me to hear Your voice clearly and continue walking in Your plan for my life. Help me to focus on You and what You have said about me in Your Word, in Jesus' name I pray. Amen.

Ephesians 1: 4 "According as he hath chosen us in him before the foundation of the world, that we should be holy and without blame before him in love:"

14

QUALIFIED

God calls willing vessels to set the captives free,

Lord, I make mistakes and have work to complete

Know that it is God who works in us for His good pleasure,

I may see myself in one way, but to God I am His special treasure.

But Lord, I am not qualified, you see Lord, they told me I am not ready

But God says I called you! I qualified you! You are my chosen vessel, fit for my use.

Focus in on My ways, as you will see that My ways are higher than your ways

And my thoughts are higher than your thoughts,

All along my child, it is Me you have always sought.

So, cling to Me and hold on to My every Word,

Over and over, it is My voice you have often heard.

Man looks at the outward appearance but remember I look at the heart

Oh, Dear Lord I am so excited now, and I can see that You were always there from the start

Lord, I now say yes, and I too answer Your call,

With anticipation and high expectations, to see like at Jericho, the walls will fall.

Oh God yes, You have called me for such a time as this,

Because of Jesus' shed Blood for me, I am qualified, and I now sit at His feet.

I now sit and receive my directions from You,

I will catapult in what You have qualified me to do.

It is not about me, my doubts, nor my fears,

It is now all about You calling me and restoring the years.

I stand boldly and proclaim Your holy grace.

Now as You use me to heal, deliver and set others free,

Because You are now calling and qualifying them for this blessed race, indeed.

A TIME OF REFLECTION

What is God calling you to do that you do not feel qualified to do?

In what ways do you feel disqualified from the assignment God has given you?

What scriptures can you stand on that shows you how God qualifies us through His mercy and grace?

LET US PRAY

Heavenly Father, my Abba Father I thank You for loving me. Help me to see myself as You see me. Thank You, Lord, that You qualify me to do all that You have called me to do. Thank You, Father, for Your Son Jesus, dying on the cross for me and You raising Him from the dead. It is because of His resurrection power that I can walk out all that Christ has called me to do. Lord, I surrender and submit to Your will, in the name of Jesus I pray. Amen.

1 Corinthians 1:26-29 "For ye see your calling, brethren, how that not many wise men after the flesh, not many mighty, not many noble, are called: But God hath chosen the foolish things of the world to confound the wise; and God hath chosen the weak things of the world to confound the things which are mighty; And base things of the world, and things which are despised, hath God chosen, yea, and things which are not, to bring to nought things that are: That no flesh should glory in his presence."

15

THE CALL

I thank my God that I answered the call

The call to do God's will upon the earth

At times it is not easy, and yes, oppositions may come

But I must persevere and allow the ministry in me to be birthed

Every time the enemy says it cannot be done

I arise to the occasion with my whole armor on

I am strong in the Lord and in the power of His might

And I decree and declare, the enemy must take flight

I stand up and know that each day His mercies are new

My calling will be done and only God I will pursue

He who began a good work in me will bring it to completion

Lives are being touched and my calling is continuously coming to pass

I denounce and remove all doubt, I press and persevere

Because I know in Christ alone, what's done for Him will surely last.

A Time of Reflection

We all have a call on our lives, so what has God called you to do? Are you already walking out your calling?

In what ways are you handling the oppositions and/or distractions concerning God's call on your life?

It is important that we daily put on the whole armor of God. What do you need to do to assure your armor is on each day?

LET US PRAY

Heavenly Father I come in the name of Jesus, thanking You for calling me. Thank You, Father, that You have given me an assignment to accomplish. Please help me to walk out this call on my life each day and that I may reach others for You. Please remove all fear, doubt and insecurity and help me to focus on my faith and my trust in You, in Jesus' name I pray. Amen.

2 Timothy 1:9 "Who hath saved us, and called us with an holy calling, not according to our works, but according to his own purpose and grace, which was given us in Christ Jesus before the world began,"

16

NOTHING CAN STOP MY PURPOSE

Nothing or no one can stop my purpose

Nothing or no one can stop God's plan

No matter the opposition, no matter the title, no matter the man

Because God said yes, I can boldly proceed

In and through Christ, I can proceed with every plan, every task, and every deed

It is better to trust in the Lord than to put my confidence in man

Oh yes, the enemy tried to block and stop me, but I was determined to go on.

It is not for the world's accolades and for man that I perform.

Because when I cried out to the Lord, He answered me and set me in a broad place.

He gently informed me that there is nothing I cannot face

God said, "You must seek My face, stay in My presence, and patiently wait as I speak

I will give you the plan as it is My Kingdom you must first seek

So, I am not cast down, and I shall not mourn,

Because God My Father is cheering me on.

I don't look to the left, I won't look to the right, for the entrance of His Word brings forth light

I have sat at His feet, and He told me the plan He made for me before I was born

I am so ready, excited and will persevere and move on.

So, I thank God for the thoughts He thinks towards me

His thoughts are as the stars in the sky and as the sand on the seashore

I must and will always focus on Him; in Him I am free.

Nothing or no one can stop His purpose for me.
65

A Time of Reflection

What do you believe your purpose is in Christ?

Regarding your purpose (God's call on you), what oppositions or stumbling blocks are you experiencing?

How can you encourage yourself in the Lord to step into your purpose and remain in your purpose?

LET US PRAY

Heavenly Father I come in the name of Jesus thanking You for creating me with a specific purpose. No matter what opposition I face, Lord You are the lifter of my head. Lord, thank You for the love You show me. I can truthfully and thankfully say Lord that nothing can stop my purpose. Each day You are taking care of me and perfecting all that concerns me, in Jesus' name I pray. Amen.

Romans 8: 28 "And we know that all things work together for good to them that love God, to them who are the called according to his purpose."

17

NOTHING CAN STOP MY PRAISE

Nothing can stop my praise
I praise God through it all
It is the name of Jesus that I call
Yes tests and trials have come
Many are the afflictions of the righteous
But God delivers us from them all
Nothing can stop my praise
Even through hurt and pain
My hands will still be raised
I continually enter His gates with thanksgiving
And I continually enter His courts with praise
I keep singing, dancing and lifting up His name
I truly give God the glory for my life will never be the
same
I praise Him with my whole heart
Because I think about how He gave me new life and a new

start

So yes, I will sing the new song He put in my heart and I
will keep my hands raised

For nothing or no one can stop my praise.

A Time of Reflection

Name something in your life that is distracting you from spending time in praise.

Describe a time in your life where praise helped you to overcome a challenging situation.

Name something you are thankful for and begin to praise God for His many blessings.

LET US PRAY

Dear Heavenly Father I come in the name of Jesus thanking You. For I am so thankful that I can praise Your name. You have given me the garment of praise for the spirit of heaviness. Please help me to focus on You and give Your name continual praise, in Jesus' name I pray. Amen.

Psalm 100:4 "Enter into his gates with thanksgiving, and into his courts with praise: be thankful unto him, and bless his name."

18

IN HIS PRESENCE

In His presence is the fullness of joy

It is where He fills every void

In His presence, burdens are removed, and yolks are destroyed

It is where I see that I am complete

I am created by Him, and I never have to compete

I yield to Him as I sit as His feet

I find complete rest and know that in Him, there is no defeat

Every longing is fulfilled as I taste and see the goodness of the Lord

He reassures me, His daughter, and He pours out to me
His Word

Of a surety, there is no other place I would rather be,

Than to be in His presence, wherein I can learn my true
identity

To my Heavenly Father I will always yield

And bask in His presence like the Samaritan woman at
the well

And I know, always, I shall be filled.

A TIME OF REFLECTION

What is a burden in your life that God can remove as you spend time in His presence?

What hollow or empty areas in your life are you trying to fill that you need to release to God?

Please spend some time in God's presence today and journal what God is placing on your heart.

LET US PRAY

Heavenly Father I come in the name of Jesus thanking You. Heavenly Father I enjoy your presence and I constantly, lovingly, experience Your love. Please help me to remember to spend time in Your presence each, and every day. Please heal me in areas where I am hurting. Help me to remember that You fill every void in my life. Thank You for being my Comforter and my Healer, in Jesus' name I pray. Amen.

Psalm 16: 11 "Thou wilt shew me the path of life: in thy presence is fulness of joy; at thy right hand there are pleasures for evermore."

19

DANCE

I dance before You Lord
As I reflect on Your love
You have turned my mourning into dancing
And gave me peace that surpasses all understanding
When I think of who You are in my life, my joy is complete
I praise You with a dance, because there is no defeat
I put the garment of praise on
The spirit of heaviness is gone
As I danced and danced, I looked down and there were no more chains
I looked up and saw Your love pouring down on me like rain
I am embracing every moment in You when I dance
I am praising You despite the circumstance
Through it all, I dance.

A TIME OF REFLECTION

Please journal about a time in your life where Jesus turned your mourning into dancing.

Please reflect upon the last time you were free in His presence and freely praised the Lord.

Please take time today to freely praise the Lord and release your burdens to Him.

LET US PRAY

Heavenly Father, I give You praise right now, and I dance before You. I lift Your name up. Father, I adore You and I need You. I give You every burden. Thank You for setting me free, in Jesus' name I pray. Amen.

Psalm 30:11-12 "Thou hast turned for me my mourning into dancing: thou hast put off my sackcloth, and girded me with gladness; To the end that my glory may sing praise to thee, and not be silent. O Lord my God, I will give thanks unto thee forever."

20

JOY

I have joy joy joy, like never before

In this new journey I am going forth

In His presence there is the fullness of joy

And at His right hand there are pleasures forevermore

The joy of the Lord is my strength

His strength is made perfect in my weakness

What He has for me is for me, and it manifests

The joy of the Lord is on the inside of me, and it stays continually

No matter the situations, no matter the circumstances

I hold the Good News of God's Word near

See, look, the victory is already here.

82

A TIME OF REFLECTION

What does encountering the joy of the Lord mean to you?

Reflect on a time that you experienced the joy of the Lord in your Life?

Joy is not based on circumstances but based on our relationship with God. What are some ways you can experience more joy in your life?

LET US PRAY

Heavenly Father I come to You in Jesus' name, thanking You for giving me joy. Thank You that there is a fullness of joy in Your presence. Please help me to spend more time being in Your presence and the enjoyable experiences of being there. Thank You that truly Your joy is my strength and I need Your strength in my life.Thank You, Lord, for supplying joy, in the name of Jesus I pray. Amen.

Nehemiah 8:10"Then he said unto them, Go your way, eat the fat, and drink the sweet, and send portions unto them for whom nothing is prepared: for this day is holy unto our Lord: neither be ye sorry; for the joy of the Lord is your strength."

21

MY HOPE

My hope never ends, it never runs out

It is strong, without a doubt

It is on God I must depend

Why am I so cast down?

And feeling defeat

When deep within I know

He won the victory

I hope in God, and I call on His name

I am transformed and will never be the same

So, every time I want to doubt

I open His Word and praises ring out

God, He truly is my only source

I trust in His Word, I'll stay the course

And when I pray in the secret place

He openly rewards

He truly holds me in His hand

That is why my hope in Him, will always stand.

A Time of Reflection

What is the one area in your life you hope will change?

What scripture will you stand on for this area to change?

Please, reflect on your past testimonies. What is an area in your life in which you held on to hope and you saw change?

LET US PRAY

Heavenly Father I come in the name of Jesus thanking You for hope. Father God, please help me to keep having hope in the midst of disappointments. Please help me to never give up and always have hope as I focus on Your Word, which strengthens me day by day. Father, I realize that there is always hope in You, in Jesus' name I pray. Amen.

Romans 5:5 "And hope maketh not ashamed; because the love of God is shed abroad in our hearts by the Holy Ghost which is given unto us."

22

MARRIAGE RESTORED

We both said, "I do" until death do we part,

But did we always put God's Word first –from the start?

Sometimes we went our own separate ways, we then began to lose heart

We became discouraged and our souls cast down

We began to move in unconnected ways with tears

But God suddenly spoke to our hearts, and He said, I will restore the years.

And we were excited and realized through Christ, our best years are ahead

There is no need to fear and there is no need to dread

For our shame, we will receive double

As we cast our cares upon the Lord and give Him our every trouble

Christ has restored us and He has made our marriage new

We will pray together, love each other, and see from God's point of view

Our marriage is better than when we started

Jesus is Lord over our marriage and truly He does heal the brokenhearted

We are at peace with each other, we are free and have a powerful testimony to share

As God lovingly rebuilds our lives together

We know that our love is unique and cannot be compared.

A TIME OF REFLECTION

Please reflect on any challenges you may be encountering in your marriage.

What is a step you can take towards putting God first in your marriage?

What are a few ways or new practices you can put in place to help your marriage grow, such as forgiveness, praying for your spouse, spending more quality time together with your spouse, etc.?

LET US PRAY

Heavenly Father, I come in the name of Jesus thanking You for my marriage. Father, You are the only one who can help my marriage be restored. With You, Lord, all things are possible. Father, please help us to overcome any challenges, obstacles, and adverse situations we are facing. Lord, I release it all over to You and declare that my marriage is blessed, sanctified, and restored, and we will have a beautiful testimony to share with others, in Jesus' name I pray. Amen.

Joel 2:25 "And I will restore to you the years that the locust hath eaten, the cankerworm, and the caterpiller, and the palmerworm, my great army which I sent among you."

23

THE SIGNIFICANCE
OF FAMILY

I truly value my family from deep within my heart

Each sibling I have loved, right from the start

Each of us has unique gifts and strengths from the Lord

When there is chaos all around, family loves you at the core

Family cares about you and for you, in the truest sense

We lovingly, devotedly want to see each other victoriously win

Others may recognize you for titles, accomplishments, and status

Deep down, family cares about you, your well-being and happiness

Even if not expressed with daily specific words, family knows and loves the authentic you

I take moments to reflect and see all of this from God's view

My family is a beautiful gift, a true blessing from the Lord

I thank my God above for every blessing, and it is Christ I adore.

A Time of Reflection

Please reflect upon your family and/or the close people in your life and thank God for bringing them in your life.

What are some of the unique strengths and gifts that the Lord has given to your various family members?

I believe that it is important to have time in life to be free among family and friends and not focus on status and having to measure up. Have you been able to focus on God and how He loves the authentic you? Is it significant for you to see the importance of those who love you for you and not for your status or accomplishments?

LET US PRAY

Heavenly Father we come in the name of Jesus lifting up Your name. Lord, I thank You for loving me at the core of who I am. I thank You for sending family and/or others in my life who love me authentically and that I can be free in You, in Jesus' name. Amen.

Psalm 133:1 "Behold, how good and how pleasant it is for brethren to dwell together in unity!"

24

TRUE FRIENDS

I thought I had many friends
Through the years we together smiled and laughed and found common ground
I thought we spoke and voiced a similar sound
Then my status was lost and the battle began
Who would be there to see me win
God showed me who was new and who was there all along
He showed me beautiful true friends to help me sing my new song
It was painful at first but I learned to depend on Him
He showed me who was in my corner as we each prayed each other through
We must see His working with new lenses and see from a kingdom of God view
God also gave me new friendships that were blossomed and birthed
We were destined to have true heavenly connections

upon the earth
And my true friends who were there all along refused to
let me quit
They refused to let me sing a sad sad song
They said stay in your new season and focus on God
alone
In your life, He only must be on the throne
My true friends old and new enjoy and accept the
authentic me
Together we pressed, persevered into true sweet victory.

A Time of Reflection

Reflect upon your friendships and ask God which friends are purposed to be in this season of your life.

Do you have like-minded friends where iron sharpens iron? Please journal regarding your friendships.

Pray, and ask God to give you newly, authentic, and blessed friendships for your destiny and friendships where you can assist others in their future endeavors and God-given destinies.

Let Us Pray

Heavenly Father, we come in Jesus' name praising Your name. Please bless my friendships, both the old and the new. Help me Dear Lord to have friendships where iron sharpens iron. Please Lord help me to have friendships that reflect Your character and love, in Jesus' name I pray. Amen.

Proverbs 17:17 "A friend loveth at all times, and a brother is born for adversity."

25

KINGDOM UNITY

We are united in Christ
God can remove all bitterness and strife
If we love God who we cannot see
We must love our brother who we see every day
Let's do all things pleasing to God, His way
Seek first the Kingdom of God
Seek His righteousness and lovingly seek God's face
His ways are higher than our ways
His thoughts are higher than our thoughts
We are united in Christ
Even when we must go our separate ways
Because our purposes call us to many parts of the earth
We are here on the earth for our destinies to be birthed
But we must love one another day by day
Because the Agape' love of Christ will pave the way
We must follow the Holy Spirit, and do what the Word
says
We are kingdom builders, united in Christ.

A TIME OF REFLECTION

What are ways God has put on your heart in which we can become more united in Christ?

How can we become more kingdom-minded and focused on seeking God?

How can we focus on the Agape' love Christ has for us and loving others more?

LET US PRAY

Heavenly Father we come in Jesus' name, thanking You for kingdom purposes. Help us Lord to love one another and focus on Your kingdom, Your will, Your ways. Help us Lord to focus on the destiny that You have for each of us. Lord, we give You all praise, glory, and honor, in Jesus' name. Amen.

Matthew 6:33 "But seek ye first the kingdom of God, and his righteousness; and all these things shall be added unto you."

26

PRUNING SEASON

Once upon a time, I had popularity with many people around
I didn't realize the many ways in which I was bound
I thought on the surface, since life was enjoyable that I was deeply trying to fill a void
I was secretly trusting in man for my destiny
Not realizing that with God I needed true identity and intimacy
God told me to obey and walk in His ways
He promised He would bring me to a new season, a new day
Every day I was pruned and drawing closer to Him
I experienced healing in His presence and a new beginning
I may not have the status and many people around

I discovered with Christ that He is the true joy I have finally found.

A TIME OF REFLECTION

What area is God pruning or trimming out of your life?

Are there any things, situations, or people in your life that God is revealing that you have placed before Him?

In what ways can you or will you start allowing Jesus to fill any voids in your life?

Let Us Pray

Heavenly Father I come in Jesus' name thanking You. Lord, please show me anything and or anyone I have placed before You. I repent and release everything to You. I thank You Lord that I am drawing closer to You. Help me Lord to obey Your ways in Jesus' name I pray. Amen.

John 15:2 "Every branch in me that beareth not fruit he taketh away: and every branch that beareth fruit, he purgeth it, that it may bring forth more fruit."

27

I ENCOURAGE YOU

I gained the victory and I broke through
It was not only for me but also, certainly for you
Don't be stagnant and don't be afraid
Through Christ, in Christ, your destiny is not delayed
Ask the Lord for your next steps
To move forward in what He has for you
Through faith, see it from God's view
He will never leave you nor forsake you
Trust Him with all your heart
See His guidance, look for His new mercies every morning
Look ahead and embrace this life's journey
I see you have made a step in the new
Take courage, be encouraged, for His ways You must continue to pursue.

A TIME OF REFLECTION

How can you go to a deeper level of trusting God?

Are there any areas where you remain stagnant? Please reflect upon how you can move forward in those areas.

What scriptures will you stand on regarding encouragement for your destiny?

LET US PRAY

Heavenly Father I come in the name of Jesus thanking You, for what I have in Christ Jesus. Help me Lord to remain encouraged in You. Help me Lord to trust You with all my heart and help me to not lean unto my own understanding. Thank You, Lord, that Your mercies are new every morning and great is Your faithfulness towards me, in Jesus' name. Amen.

Proverbs 3:5-6 "Trust in the Lord with all thine heart; and lean not unto thine own understanding. In all thy ways acknowledge him, and he shall direct thy paths."

28

THE WALLS CAME DOWN

The walls came down
The walls came down
I am in the Promised Land
I am walking in freedom and a promised destiny
Now God's will, I now clearly see
Every enemy has been defeated
The negative cycles in my life are no longer repeated
Low self-esteem and timidity are not mine
In an old wine skin, how can I pour in new wine
The walls have already come down
And now in Christ, I am a new creation you see
I must continue this path, and speak only victory
Don't identify me with my past
My relationship and newness in Christ will forever last
You may still see it and compare it with the old
The truth in Christ has now been experienced and told

The walls are down, and I have now entered His rest
I have my inheritance in Him and because of Christ
I now have the best!

A TIME OF REFLECTION

What walls need to come down in your life so that you can freely walk in your relationship with Christ?

What negative cycle in your life have you overcome?

Write a declaration of victory regarding one area in your life.

LET US PRAY

Heavenly Father I come in the name of Jesus. I thank You that the walls that separate me from the sweet victories in life are coming down. Help me Lord to focus on my relationship with You. Help me to realize each day that the enemy is defeated, and I walk in sweet victory, in Jesus' name I pray. Amen.

Joshua 6:20 "So the people shouted when the priests blew with the trumpets: and it came to pass, when the people heard the sound of the trumpet, and the people shouted with a great shout, that the wall fell down flat, so that the people went up into the city, every man straight before him, and they took the city."

29

ON THE OTHER SIDE

There is victory on the other side, it is in Christ that I hide

You see I have already broken through, I am in the unknown yes I am in the new

The pressure is deep, I have taken a big leap

All I feel is pain

But God asks, Can you anticipate the abundance of rain?

I feel alone as I have stepped out on faith

I must trust God, I must run the race.

I must keep moving and keep pressing forward

I must use my shield of faith

I must use my weapon, the Word of God, my sword

Like God told Joshua I must be strong and courageous

I must meditate on the Word day and night

I must walk by faith and not by sight

Just like the Israelites crossed the Red Sea

I too have moved past the wilderness
I must get to the Promised Land, my land of victory
The walls must come down and I hear the trumpet sound
I am now on the other side
Here is my freedom, here is my victory
God is my Banner, God is my guide
Oh yes, there is glorious victory over on the other side.

A TIME OF REFLECTIONS

How are you using your shield of faith? Name one scripture that you use to quench the fiery darts of the enemy.

Through Christ what do you envision as your Promised Land –your place of victory?

What is one way you can be strong and courageous when the enemy attacks?

LET US PRAY

Heavenly Father I love You and thank You for victory on the other side. Thank You for leading me and guiding me. Please help me to continue meditating on Your Word -both day and night. Thank You Lord for fighting my battles in Jesus' name I pray. Amen.

Joshua 1:9 "Have not I commanded thee? Be strong and of a good courage; be not afraid, neither be thou dismayed: for the Lord thy God is with thee whithersoever thou goest."

30

THE FAVOR OF GOD STEPPED IN

I was turned down for a promotion and a wonderful opportunity in life

I saw no victory, no way in sight

I cried and struggled and endured the fight

I turned to others for answers concerning my ordeal. And then I asked...

Why Lord did I not get a call?

You know Lord, I don't want to fail or fall

So, I cast my burden over onto God

And I prayed earnestly in faith

That is when my sweet change began to take place

Suddenly God's favor stepped right in

And when I began to see my season, I knew I would win

I had to learn and realize that His favor surrounds me like a shield

Yes, to Jesus the Christ I now wholeheartedly yield

It was not by power nor by might

But when I turned it over and gave to Jesus my fight

He supplied my every need according to His riches in glory

You see, He is the author and the finisher of my faith

Continually, consistently, daily, He is the author of my story.

A TIME OF REFLECTION

Describe a time in your life where you know it was God's favor that turned a situation around for you.

What opportunity are you believing God to come to pass in your life?

What are ways in which you are relying on God's grace and His timely favor through your faith, for the opportunity to come?

LET US PRAY

Heavenly Father I come in Jesus' name thanking You and relying on You. Thank You for Your favor. Your favor surrounds me as a shield every day. Please help me to remember that You are keeping me, and I have no need to worry. Thank You for every opportunity You give me to walk out Your will in my life, in Jesus' name I pray. Amen.

Psalm 5:12 "For thou, Lord, wilt bless the righteous; with favour wilt thou compass him as with a shield."

31

PUSH FORWARD

When you are afraid and you feel stagnant
You must push forward, trust in what God has in store for you
Remember the dream He placed down on the inside
Remember always that in Him you must abide
Rise Up! Leave your comfort zone
And remember to depend on Jesus who sits on the throne
Go boldly to the throne of grace
Call upon Him, and always always, seek His will, His face
Push forward and forget those things which are behind
Press toward the mark of the high calling in Him
Although it may look unclear or uncertain at first, remember my friend, you win
You know, He always causes us to triumph
And He reminds us of our dreams, so that His plans can be birthed
Push forward into the things of God and please, have no regrets

When you live, love and depend on Him, God will never forget

He will never forget your labor of love

So, please, keep your mind on heavenly things above.

A TIME OF REFLECTION

What is truly keeping you from pushing forward?

What dream did God put on the inside of you that you would love to see birthed?

Please write down at least one goal towards accomplishing your dream.

LET US PRAY

Heavenly Father thank You for helping me to push forward. I am excited because I know Dear Lord You have so much in store for me. Help me to focus on the dreams You have placed down on the inside of me. Please help me Lord to stay in Your will for my life as I hear from You, as I hear from Your dwelling place in Heaven each day. In Jesus' name I pray. Amen

Philippians 3:13-14 "Brethren, I count not myself to have apprehended: but this one thing I do, forgetting those things which are behind, and reaching forth unto those things which are before, I press toward the mark for the prize of the high calling of God in Christ Jesus."

32

YOUR HEALING IS COMPLETE

You may ask Lord, does healing belong to me?

Know my friend, that He redeemed you and purchased your healing on Calvary

Your healing is complete, receive it in His Word

Stand on every promise and every encouraging Word that you have heard

Cast all your cares on Jesus and remember to only believe

Speak to every mountain in your life and remember His promises are Yes! and Amen!

You are already healed, restored and free

Think of the finished work of the cross and see your healing as done and complete

Think of blind Bartimaeus, the man at the Pool of Bethesda and so many miracles Jesus had done

You must know that even when you can't see the manifestation, He has victory already won

Remember that Jesus went about showing compassion and healing all manner of disease

Jesus accomplished your salvation, freedom, and healing in His name

Your healing is complete, and God's Word never changes, it remains the same.

A Time of Reflection

Are you believing for healing in any area of your life?

Please, reflect upon your testimony, a time in your life where God brought healing to you in your body, in a relationship, etc., and spend time in giving Him some praise for the healing.

Please reflect upon a Bible account that speaks to your heart regarding God's healing.

LET US PRAY

Heavenly Father I come in Jesus' name thanking You for my healing. Lord, You are my Healer and I trust You. You alone are God. I thank You, Lord that it is by Your stripes, that I am healed and that I am made whole. Please help my heart to stay encouraged, in Jesus' name. Amen.

Matthew 4:23 "And Jesus went about all Galilee, teaching in their synagogues, preaching the gospel of the kingdom, and healing all kinds of sickness and all kinds of disease among the people."

33

CELEBRATE THE VICTORY

It's a celebration
It's a new day
Release your praise
Lift up His name
Your joy and victory remains
God has done exceedingly and abundantly above all we
ask or think
Restoration is here
Your vision has appeared
Dance and shout and look ahead
You have abundant life in Christ
Embrace His loving kindness, his mercy and grace
Enjoy every moment as you seek His face
It is celebration
It is a new day

His great grace is upon you
In great anticipation, let God have His way.

A TIME OF REFLECTION

What is the situation or vision God has given you in which you need to take a moment to celebrate in your life?

What is God showing you that needs restoration in your life. Is it your marriage, relationships, your prayer life, etc?

Reflect upon what an abundant life in Christ will look like for you, personally. Please journal what God has put on your heart.

LET US PRAY

Heavenly Father I thank You for the victory. Please help me to celebrate all that You are doing in my life. Please help me to know and understand the vision You have for me. Lord I am excited to enjoy every moment with You in this abundant life You have given me, in Jesus' name I pray. Amen.

1 Corinthians 15:57 "But thanks be to God, which giveth us the victory through our Lord Jesus Christ."

34

MANIFESTATIONS

Daughter, know, it is already done
At Calvary, I finished the work on the cross
I have reestablished and restored all that was lost
Your healing, your deliverance, your ministry
Is manifesting in me
It is already accomplished in Heaven above
Call forth your manifestation and bask in my love
What do you now stand in need of
You must know that every need is already met
Even if you haven't seen the manifestation yet
By my stripes you were healed and with the Holy Spirit
you are sealed
Manifestation time is here
Look up! Your victory has appeared!

A Time of Reflection

What are you believing to see God manifest in your life?

What needs to be restored and healed in your life?

What scriptures are you standing on as you trust God to believe?

LET US PRAY

Heavenly Father I come in the name of Jesus thanking You for manifestations. Thank You Lord for Your promises. Lord, I trust You. You are the only one who knows what I stand in need of. Lord I will not give up on what You have promised me, in Jesus' name. Amen.

1 John 5:14-16 "Now this is the confidence that we have in Him, that if we ask anything according to His will, He hears us. And if we know that He hears us, whatever we ask, we know that we have the petitions that we have asked of Him."

35

THE BEST IS YET TO COME

The best is yet to come
Don't be discouraged
You are so close
You have already won
His favor surrounds You as a shield
To the Holy Spirit you must yield
Day break has come and your new season is here
Keep pressing forward and to Jesus draw near
Your latter days will be greater than your former
So keep looking ahead
Do not fear and do not dread
Your best days are ahead
The best is yet to come.

A Time of Reflection

Please reflect upon your relationship with the Lord and how you can draw even closer to Him.

Are there any fears that you need to overcome? What scriptures are you going to stand on to overcome those fears?

What are you believing God for that will be a part of your best days ahead?

LET US PRAY

Heavenly Father I come in the name of Jesus thanking You and that I can love on You. Help me Lord to yield to the Holy Spirit. Father help me to reflect on the belief that the best is yet to come, in Jesus' name. Amen.

Job 8:7 "Though your beginning was small, Yet your latter end would increase abundantly."

MY FAVORITE PSALM FOR DAILY PROTECTION

PSALM 91

He who dwells in the secret place of the Most High

Shall abide under the shadow of the Almighty.

I will say of the Lord, "He is my refuge and my fortress;

My God, in Him I will trust."

Surely, He shall deliver you from the snare of the fowler

And from the perilous pestilence.

He shall cover you with His feathers,

And under His wings you shall take refuge.

His truth shall be your shield and buckler.

You shall not be afraid of the terror by night,

Nor of the arrow that flies by day,

Nor of the pestilence that walks in darkness,

Nor of the destruction that lays waste at noonday.

A thousand may fall at your side,

And ten thousand at your right hand;

But it shall not come near you.

Only with your eyes shall you look,

And see the reward of the wicked.

Because you have made the Lord, who is my refuge,

Even the Most High, your dwelling place,

No evil shall befall you,

Nor shall any plague come near your dwelling.

For He shall give His angels charge over you,

To keep you in all your ways.

In their hands they shall bear you up,

Lest you dash your foot against a stone.

You shall tread upon the lion and the cobra,

The young lion and the serpent you shall trample underfoot.

"Because he has set his love upon Me, therefore I will deliver him.

I will set him on high because he has known My name.

He shall call upon Me, and I will answer him.

I will be with him in trouble;

I will deliver him and honor him.

With long life I will satisfy him,

And show him My salvation."

Salvation Prayer

If you have never made Jesus the Lord of your life, you can invite Him into your heart right now.

Prayer for Salvation

Heavenly Father please forgive me for all my sins. Jesus, please come into my heart and be Savior and Lord over my life. I believe that You died and rose from the dead for me. God, You said in Your Word that if I would confess Jesus as my Savior and Lord, I would be saved. Jesus, have your way in my life. I give my life to You now, in the mighty name of Jesus I pray. Amen

Romans 10:9-10

"That if thou shalt confess with thy mouth the Lord Jesus, and shalt believe in thine heart that God hath raised him from the dead, thou shalt be saved. For with the heart man believeth unto righteousness; and with the mouth confession is made unto salvation."